# Desultory reflections on police: with an essay on the means of preventing crimes and amending criminals. By William Blizard, F.S.A. Surgeon of the Honourable Artillery-Company, &c.

William Blizard

*Desultory reflections on police: with an essay on the means of preventing crimes and amending criminals. By William Blizard, F.S.A. Surgeon of the Honourable Artillery-Company, &c.*
Blizard, William, Sir
ESTCID: T000916
Reproduction from British Library

London : printed, by Baker and Galabin, for C. Dilly, 1785.
vii,[1],83,[1]p.,plate ; 8°

Eighteenth Century
Collections Online
Print Editions

**Gale ECCO Print Editions**

Relive history with *Eighteenth Century Collections Online*, now available in print for the independent historian and collector. This series includes the most significant English-language and foreign-language works printed in Great Britain during the eighteenth century, and is organized in seven different subject areas including literature and language; medicine, science, and technology; and religion and philosophy. The collection also includes thousands of important works from the Americas.

The eighteenth century has been called "The Age of Enlightenment." It was a period of rapid advance in print culture and publishing, in world exploration, and in the rapid growth of science and technology – all of which had a profound impact on the political and cultural landscape. At the end of the century the American Revolution, French Revolution and Industrial Revolution, perhaps three of the most significant events in modern history, set in motion developments that eventually dominated world political, economic, and social life.

In a groundbreaking effort, Gale initiated a revolution of its own: digitization of epic proportions to preserve these invaluable works in the largest online archive of its kind. Contributions from major world libraries constitute over 175,000 original printed works. Scanned images of the actual pages, rather than transcriptions, recreate the works *as they first appeared.*

Now for the first time, these high-quality digital scans of original works are available via print-on-demand, making them readily accessible to libraries, students, independent scholars, and readers of all ages.

For our initial release we have created seven robust collections to form one the world's most comprehensive catalogs of $18^{th}$ century works.

*Initial Gale ECCO Print Editions collections include:*

> *History and Geography*
> Rich in titles on English life and social history, this collection spans the world as it was known to eighteenth-century historians and explorers. Titles include a wealth of travel accounts and diaries, histories of nations from throughout the world, and maps and charts of a world that was still being discovered. Students of the War of American Independence will find fascinating accounts from the British side of conflict.

*Social Science*
Delve into what it was like to live during the eighteenth century by reading the first-hand accounts of everyday people, including city dwellers and farmers, businessmen and bankers, artisans and merchants, artists and their patrons, politicians and their constituents. Original texts make the American, French, and Industrial revolutions vividly contemporary.

*Medicine, Science and Technology*
Medical theory and practice of the 1700s developed rapidly, as is evidenced by the extensive collection, which includes descriptions of diseases, their conditions, and treatments. Books on science and technology, agriculture, military technology, natural philosophy, even cookbooks, are all contained here.

*Literature and Language*
Western literary study flows out of eighteenth-century works by Alexander Pope, Daniel Defoe, Henry Fielding, Frances Burney, Denis Diderot, Johann Gottfried Herder, Johann Wolfgang von Goethe, and others. Experience the birth of the modern novel, or compare the development of language using dictionaries and grammar discourses.

*Religion and Philosophy*
The Age of Enlightenment profoundly enriched religious and philosophical understanding and continues to influence present-day thinking. Works collected here include masterpieces by David Hume, Immanuel Kant, and Jean-Jacques Rousseau, as well as religious sermons and moral debates on the issues of the day, such as the slave trade. The Age of Reason saw conflict between Protestantism and Catholicism transformed into one between faith and logic -- a debate that continues in the twenty-first century.

*Law and Reference*
This collection reveals the history of English common law and Empire law in a vastly changing world of British expansion. Dominating the legal field is the *Commentaries of the Law of England* by Sir William Blackstone, which first appeared in 1765. Reference works such as almanacs and catalogues continue to educate us by revealing the day-to-day workings of society.

*Fine Arts*
The eighteenth-century fascination with Greek and Roman antiquity followed the systematic excavation of the ruins at Pompeii and Herculaneum in southern Italy; and after 1750 a neoclassical style dominated all artistic fields. The titles here trace developments in mostly English-language works on painting, sculpture, architecture, music, theater, and other disciplines. Instructional works on musical instruments, catalogs of art objects, comic operas, and more are also included.

**The BiblioLife Network**

This project was made possible in part by the BiblioLife Network (BLN), a project aimed at addressing some of the huge challenges facing book preservationists around the world. The BLN includes libraries, library networks, archives, subject matter experts, online communities and library service providers. We believe every book ever published should be available as a high-quality print reproduction; printed on-demand anywhere in the world. This insures the ongoing accessibility of the content and helps generate sustainable revenue for the libraries and organizations that work to preserve these important materials.

The following book is in the "public domain" and represents an authentic reproduction of the text as printed by the original publisher. While we have attempted to accurately maintain the integrity of the original work, there are sometimes problems with the original work or the micro-film from which the books were digitized. This can result in minor errors in reproduction. Possible imperfections include missing and blurred pages, poor pictures, markings and other reproduction issues beyond our control. Because this work is culturally important, we have made it available as part of our commitment to protecting, preserving, and promoting the world's literature.

**GUIDE TO FOLD-OUTS MAPS and OVERSIZED IMAGES**

The book you are reading was digitized from microfilm captured over the past thirty to forty years. Years after the creation of the original microfilm, the book was converted to digital files and made available in an online database.

In an online database, page images do not need to conform to the size restrictions found in a printed book. When converting these images back into a printed bound book, the page sizes are standardized in ways that maintain the detail of the original. For large images, such as fold-out maps, the original page image is split into two or more pages

Guidelines used to determine how to split the page image follows:

• Some images are split vertically; large images require vertical and horizontal splits.
• For horizontal splits, the content is split left to right.
• For vertical splits, the content is split from top to bottom.
• For both vertical and horizontal splits, the image is processed from top left to bottom right.

# DESULTORY REFLECTIONS ON POLICE:

## WITH AN ESSAY

On the Means of PREVENTING CRIMES
and AMENDING CRIMINALS.

By WILLIAM BLIZARD, F. S. A.
Surgeon of the Honourable Artillery-Company, &c.

---

Prodesse quàm conspici.

---

LONDON:
Printed, by BAKER and GALABIN,
For C. DILLY, in the POULTRY.
M.DCC.LXXXV.

TO

THE RIGHT HONOURABLE THE

LORD-MAYOR,

THE

ALDERMEN,

RECORDER,

SHERIFFS,

AND

COMMON-COUNCIL,

OF THE

City of London,

IN FULL ASSURANCE OF THEIR ATTENTION

TO EVERY SINCERE ENDEAVOUR

FOR PROMOTING PUBLIC PEACE AND PROSPERITY,

THESE

REFLECTIONS

ARE MOST RESPECTFULLY INSCRIBED,

BY

WILLIAM BLIZARD.

# INTRODUCTION.

WHEN the enemies of this country, in the late war, avowed their intention of invasion, many gentlemen of character and property, in the city, armed, and formed themselves into a company, under the title of THE LONDON MILITARY FOOT-ASSOCIATION. The outrages, that have happened since that period, evince how necessary the presence of such a body, in the metropolis, would have been, in case our enemies had rashly ventured on the execution of their design. I shall ever glory in having been a member of this volunteer-corps from its institution. When folly and fanaticism, enemies of every country! produced the memorable riots in June, 1780, these gentlemen stood forth; and from that period have been known to their fellow-citizens.——— In the year 1781, most of the members incorporated themselves with the Honourable Artillery-Company, and the Association ceased.

This Company, thus recruited, have followed the example of the London Militaty Foot-Association, *in supporting the civil power in the maintaining of* Peace *and* Order and their services have been frequently required by the chief magistrate of this city.

The observations I made on those occasions I thought too important to be withholden from the public, and some of them I communicated, in a morning-paper, under the signature of Curtius.

The King has been ever a friend to virtue and justice, we have *now* a minister, virtuous as well as able and active, and it is understood to be the intention of government to form a plan for the security and happiness of the community. This, therefore, is undoubtedly the time for good subjects to come forward with every fact that can possibly illustrate the history of crimes, and advance so desirable an end

The *sole* views, then, of this little work, are, to authenticate facts that have been before published,

to

to add others yet more extraordinary; and thus to endeavour, in some degree, to assist magistrates in their laudable undertakings, and, if possible, promote public virtue.

My professional duties allowed me but little time for the execution of my design; and, on looking over the sheets, I have remarked many inaccuracies, but none that affect my meaning. The truth of the whole is incontrovertible, and I am more anxious concerning its influence on the minds of my readers than for my own reputation as a writer: the former may happily produce some good to mankind, the latter can be of little consequence to myself, and of none to the world.

Lime-Street,
September 10, 1785.

LETTERS

# LETTERS

On the Subject of

# POLICE.

---

## LETTER I.

TO ****** ******.

SIR,

YOU have been pleased to express a pleasure in hearing me relate some of the observations, made on the many occasions that I accompanied parties of the London Military Foot-Association for the apprehension of thieves and other descriptions of bad men. You now desire me to write down my reflections on what I have seen. I shall obey your command. But, although, my good sir, you might be entertained with the account of the various scenes that were presented to us in our excursions, because they were truly extraordinary, and such as in your walks of life you could never have obferved, yet, when you fhall be led to reflect with me on the nature and magnitude of iniquity in this town, you will feel yourfelf very differently affected When VICE fhall appear to be the foundation of plans and fyftems bearing the fair titles of *virtue* and *juftice*, you will fhudder, and exclaim, *It is too much!*

I remember a faying of your's, " that no defign " could be juft, which required, in the execution, " the agency of bad men " I moft fincerely affent to the principle, but mankind feem, frequently, to be governed by a very different opinion.

*Set a thief to catch a thief* is a proverbial faying, which, like many others, is very apt to miflead through an affociation of ideas, and occafion a conduct hurtful to the peace and intereft of fociety, There are no concerns, that are founded in rectitude, but may be executed by *honeft men*; this is an axiom that religion and the foundeft human policy will defend How repugnant to it is the practice of fome of the magiftrates in the vicinity of this town! daily experience proves, that *intereft* is their governing principle.

The

The chains of connection and benefit, in many public concerns, would afford curious speculation to the moralist, and the historian of the ways of men. Observations, for instance, authorize the supposition, that the clerk is oftentimes the *medium* between the magistrate and the runner, or constable, and the keepers of houses of entertainment the links between the runner and the thief. There are, however, varieties in this chain of iniquity, and there are reasons for thinking, that sometimes the magistrate is not placed at so handsome a distance from the thief.

By this communication, these magistrates obtain a knowledge of thieves and their haunts in these great cities. The information is procured by means dishonourable, and the application of it is not consonant to the rules of virtue and justice Their interest and the support of their credit with the world demand, that the vengeance of the law should sometimes be executed on deluded culprits. But, when justice is satisfied, and a wretch dies, can he be said to fall a sacrifice more to his own evil propensities than to the wickedness of these men? who might have checked him in his wild career, have broken up the nurseries where his follies became vices, and where these were cherished into crimes dreadfully degrading to human nature!

A plan of police, founded in strict honour and justice, might have all the advantages of information of the places of rendezvous of bad men; and these are the first great objects of attention. In regard to minute circumstances respecting criminals, such as are found subservient and necessary to the temporizing thief-taking system of our modern magistrates, and which can only be obtained by a too intimate acquaintance with bad men, these would not be required in a police founded in pure intentions. There should be no farther intimacy, with such a description of men, than what is judged absolutely necessary for their reformation and the security of the public.

The spirited and well-directed exertions of firm and honest magistrates would soon convince mankind, that, in proceedings against breakers of the laws, as well as in all other human affairs, *honesty is the best policy*, and, therefore, it is not right to *set a thief to catch a thief*.

The

The notion, of the necessity of the services of depraved and hardened men, has been carried a step farther than *setting a thief to catch a thief*, for it appears, that *thieves are employed to look after thieves*. What would the good Mr HANWAY say to this, who is labouring continually to render the period of captivity of criminals a time of reflection, of instruction, and amendment?

On the 12th of August, 1781, advice was sent, to the Armory-House of the \*Honourable Artillery-Company, of a dangerous riot in Wood-street compter. I accompanied the late Sir BARNARD TURNER and Captain † SMITH, with the grenadier company, in order to quell this disturbance. Never was I a witness of such dreadful depravity! On entering the prison, we were informed, that a turnkey had been stabbed in the affray. I was immediately

---

\* The gentlemen of the London Military Foot-Association had at that time incorporated themselves with the Honourable Artillery-Company.

† Now major of the Honourable Artillery-Company.

mediately conducted to him; but, finding he had chirurgical affiftance, and that the wound was flight, I rejoined my company. I will not hurt your feelings by relating the circumftances of the behaviour of the rioters. One, like Beelzebub, eminent among his infernal fpirits, ftood foremoft, and declared himfelf the man who had attempted to murder the turnkey, and juftified and gloried in the deed; adding, "*He was a thief like himfelf*; and that, if "his own FATHER had ferved him as he had done, "he would have ftabbed him in the like manner!"— It did truly appear, that the turnkey was then a prifoner for a theft. The rioters were conducted, with fome difficulty and danger, to a dungeon beneath the prifon, whence we were obliged to retreat, walking backwards, with bayonets in our hands, for they were not difmayed, but continued to declare their intention of deftroying us.

I heard nothing of this wounded man till once on a vifit to a gentleman, in Newgate, imprifoned on account of an affair of honour, *as it is called*; and, paffing along one of the areas, feveral of the prifoners

ers attempted to huſtle me * A turnkey came to me, but appeared to be exceedingly terrified, and not in a ſtate to afford me any aſſiſtance. Happily, I extricated myſelf from them, and got to the place of confinement of the gentleman. I began to remark, that I had never ſeen ſuch brutality but once before, and related ſome of the circumſtances of the riot at the compter, when the turnkey who had followed me, and was ſtanding by, ſaid, " I am the man, ſir, " who was ſtabbed," at the ſame time pulling up his ſhirt to give me proof of the truth of what he ſaid by the ſcar from the wound.

Surely no one can ſeriouſly think, that true ſpirit and firmneſs can be found in thieves. The courage, calmneſs, and fortitude, of integrity,† muſt ever be
ſuperior

---

* This was the firſt expreſſion of a very dreadful diſturbance which happened there the ſame day.

† Juſtum et tenacem propoſiti virum,
Non civium ardor prava jubentium,
 Non vultus inſtantis tyranni,
 Mente quatit ſolida, neque Auſter,
Dux inquieti turbidus Adriæ,
Nec fulminantis magna manus Jovis.
      Hor.

superior to what can possibly be derived from habits of wickedness.

The keepers of prisons may, doubtless, be good men. Let them, then, as possessing integrity, and as worthy citizens, consider of how much importance it is to the security and happiness of society, not to mention higher motives and obligations, that their prisoners be so looked after as that they may not be made worse, if not mended, by confinement, that the prisons, in short, be not rendered evils of the most pernicious kind, instead of benefits, to the community.

The practice, of appointing criminals to superintend prisoners, must be productive of a thousand bad effects!

The goodness of your own heart, my honoured friend, may perhaps lead you to think, that my suspicions, respecting the conduct of some magistrates, are expressed in rather too strong terms. You will shortly hold another opinion. You must hear all my tales of these gentlemen, and of the fraternity of thieves, before you decide. Were I, at once, to draw you the strong face of wickedness, you might

think

think it not correct, and turn from it with disgust. In my next, however, I shall venture to present you with a pretty bold picture of a trading justice.

I am, sir, &c.

# LETTER II.

### TO ****** ******.

SIR,

IF men were to reflect on the nature of the human mind in a depraved state, and the consequences of actions flowing from principles of injustice and vice, they would certainly on no occasion confide in them whose conduct they did not believe to be founded in rectitude. Why is it, sir, that men can look around them, and see all the visible works of the creation declaring a regular dependence of causes and effects, and yet attend not to the influence of virtue and vice? Surely there is a strange dislike to the exercise of the brightest faculty of man, his REASON! He will tremble at the sight of a blazing star, lest it portend evil; but he will see wickedness, in every part, rearing its baneful head, unheedful of the effects, which will follow as regularly and certainly as in the natural world, unless prevented by the superior power of virtuous exertions.

ORDER is nature's universal theme;
Unheeded only in the ways of men.
Let comets shine, or thunder shake the heav'ns,
Or all the skies a placid aspect wear
Yet VICE foretels a nation's certain fall,
Distraction still awaits a trait'rous heart,
And ruin hovers o'er a tyrant's head!

It may, then, be asked, from what causes this nation now exists? Because, through the will of Providence, the quantity of evil has not yet, in its effects, over-balanced the good. But let us not think ourselves secure. That nation must be in great danger, in which lawless men constitute a considerable part of the community. But so it is, at this day, in England. It is, therefore, the duty of every man to consider of means of preventing crimes, reclaiming criminals, and restraining the incorrigible from acts of violence and injustice.

Some contend, " that none but men without cha-
" racter would engage in the office of apprehending
" thieves,

" thieves, or that of taking charge of them in con-
" finement." Admitting the truth of this remark, who must not be shocked at it? Offices, which, executed by worthy men, would have been esteemed honourable, because of the highest importance to mankind, are now deemed otherwise, from the folly and baseness of men, in preferring rogues and outcasts of society! But I deny the fact, that honest men would not engage in these undertakings. Remove the obnoxious persons, and determine to employ none but men whose characters are fair, and such would be always ready.

How many benefits would flow from only this regulation in the practices of magistrates and superintendents of prisons! Suppose, for example, subservient to a plan of police, every keeper of a prison were to keep a register of occurrences, and that the several deputies and turnkeys, being men of probity, were to endeavour, by honourable means, to obtain information of gangs of thieves, house-breakers, &c. their dwellings, relations, associates, places of rendezvous, &c. &c. What schemes of villany

might

might be explored, and, through the activity of magistrates, be prevented perpetration! The observations, too, of these persons, of the circumstances and fates of many hapless wretches who had been within their walls, might, in favourable moments, be usefully applied, in the way of warning to their miserable prisoners.

Shocking reverse! now thieves have the magnitude of their crimes diminished in their sight, in observing criminals, like themselves, raised into an office of trust and authority. With what firmness can the thief in office act? with what weight admonish? How, in short, can the discipline of a prison be maintained without principle, without confidence? Alas! there is no discipline in a prison, for within its walls the institutes of God and men seem to be totally disregarded. The arch-enemy of mankind could not have suggested a more perfect mode of completion, in all the arts of wickedness, than by congregating malefactors of every description within our prisons! Is it not, my revered friend, curious to observe, what wondrous pains are taken to prepare for

the

the next world a poor wretch who is condemned to die? His foul, in a moment, is become of great value, and his faith, confeffion, and falvation, are objects of high regard. The world, too, it is thought, may, at the laft, derive a little good from him; and the diftracted creature is harrowed with queftions concerning his crimes and affociates. ——— If equal pains had been taken to prevent his corruption, and progrefs in vice, when he *firſt* became an inhabitant of a prifon; if he had been brought to folitary reflection, had been warned by example, and taken from evil communication, he would have been refcued from an ignominious death, have lived obedient to the laws, an ufeful member of fociety.

Let us now turn to the means employed for the fecuring of infractors of the laws. It is afferted, " that honeft men will not undertake this " bufinefs." Then certainly we muft keep up the race of rogues, for we have a deal of work for them But, fir, to be ferious if men of honour and fpirit will not engage in the work of apprehending dangerous members of fociety, from dread of disgrace,

disgrace, because magistrates, wanting either wisdom or integrity, have made bad men their instruments of folly or wickedness, it is high time that a different practice were established; that other sentiments might take place in the minds of honest citizens. While the heart retains its purity, information and advice may produce wonderful effects. If the practice condemned had arisen altogether from an erroneous notion, we might have hoped, that reason and experience would, at some period, produce an alteration. But this is not the case; it is founded in positive injustice and wickedness. The following account was given to me by a gentleman of strict honour and veracity, who is ready to attest the narrative. It justifies my assertion of a chain of connection between some magistrates and thieves, and proves, that the extermination of the one is as necessary as of the other.

" Some time in the autumn of the year 1780, I
" was stopped and robbed, by three armed men, in
" the road to Islington Not having made an appli-
" cation to any magistrate, I was surprised, when,
" early the next morning, one of Justice B***'s
                                            " constables

"constables called on me, and told me, 'that he
"understood I had been robbed the preceding
"evening, that they had taken up three men, and
"that he wished me to go and see whether they were
"the persons who had stopped me.' I went with
"them, and met, at the justice's house, several peo-
"ple who had lately been robbed near the spot I had
"been, and most likely by the party that had rifled
"me. The men they had apprehended, however,
"were not the thieves, but proved themselves to be
"honest and industrious people. They were there-
"fore discharged, but were ordered to pay one shil-
"ling each to the justice's clerk before their depar-
"ture. Upon their declaring their incapacity, not
"having a farthing in their pockets, the justice
"would not set them at liberty, and, it appeared,
"they would actually have been sent to prison, if I
"had not supplied them with the sum required. This
"affair being settled, one of the constables (the
"same who had been with me) told me, 'if I
"durst venture with him, he would shew me the
"men who had robbed me.' I asked the magis-
"trate's opinion about accompanying him. He ob-
"served,

" ferved, ' that it was very likely his men might
" take me to a place where the robbers might be ap-
" prehended.' I, therefore, agreed to attend the
" man, and, the next morning being appointed, I
" met him and another conftable  They led me to
" a place, in *Chick-lane*, where we feized a man,
" whom I then believed to be one of thofe who had
" robbed me. He was immediately carried before
" the juftice, and I depofed, ' That I firmly fuf-
" pected and believed him to be one of the men who
" had ftopped and robbed me.' The juftice repeat-
" edly afked me, in terms of great urgency, ' if I
" could not fwear pofitively to him?' I replied
" ' No; but that, if thofe people were fent for who
" had been there the day before, perhaps their evi-
" dence might be more pofitive than mine.' He
" then faid, ' he believed I muft be in a miftake,'
" and afked me, ' if I would accept of bail,' and
" offered two of his conftables for that purpofe.
" Perceiving that I hefitated, he defired me to with-
" draw with him, and then told me, ' that his men
" had affured him that this was not the perfon, that
" I need not fcruple taking the bail that had been of-
" fered,

" fered, for I might be sure it was safe; and,
" that this man would, perhaps, lead him to a disco-
" very of the persons really concerned.' Highly in-
" censed, yet not knowing what other measure to
" take, I made no objection the bail was accept-
" ed, and the man set at liberty, and, what was not
" a little curious, his bail were the very men who
" had apprehended him! These men spake to me,
" as I was leaving the office, to this effect: ' You
" were certainly very much deceived, sir, respecting
" this man; though, to be sure, he is a thief, and
" has not left the ballast-lighter above a month;
" but he does not yet do any thing so *considerable* as
" your affair was; he is only in a *low* way yet, such
" as picking of pockets and robbing of carts; and,
" at the very time you were robbed, he was robbing
" waggons in another part.' — I interrupted them
" here, by asking them, ' as they knew this, why
" they did not prosecute him?' They smiled at me,
" in a seemingly-contemptuous manner, and made
" use of these particular words ' Oh! God bless
" you, sir; it is our interest to let *little* fish go, that
" we may get *great* ones!' This thoroughly satis-
" fied

"fied me as to the principles of their conduct. I
"went next morning to the justice's house; and,
"an *alibi* having been so *clearly* proved to me, I very
"readily acknowledged I must have been in a mis-
"take. The prisoner was accordingly discharged.
"Tired with such villany, it may be supposed I re-
"fused to have any thing more to do with the justice
"or his *catchers of great fish*.

"This event being at the distance of five years, I
"may have omitted some circumstances, but what I
"have related are facts of so remarkably infamous a
"nature as not easily to be forgotten, and of the
"truth of which I am certain."

Make your own comments on this relation, and then, if you can, exult, as you have been used to do, in the security and liberty of an honest British subject, in the impartial administration of justice; and the purity and uprightness of our magistrates!

Yet, my good friend, some of the brightest and most amiable characters are invested with the power of magistracy and it is an evil of the most alarming kind, that these gentlemen will not come forward in exertions respecting offenders, lest their fair names should be sullied through the baseness of men who disgrace the title of magistrate.

I am, &c.

## LETTER III.

TO ****** ******.

SIR,

IF to be active and firm in the defence and protection of our country, and all that is valuable, against the attacks of foreign foes, be noble and praise-worthy, why should it not be esteemed equally so to detect and oppose the domestic disturbers of the peace of good citizens, the lawless ravagers of property, and destroyers of lives?

Estimate the different services by a comparison of the nature of the evils. The domestic enemy is a secret and insidious one, who defies the laws of his country, who acts under no *lex gentium*, or rules of honour or humanity. The foreign enemy openly meets you in the field, and a battle, in which there is mutual danger, decides the contest. If the one fight to obtain possession of the kingdom, the other takes away property and lives, without which the kingdom cannot be defended. The end of war is to live in peace, and the security of this blessing is deserving of the most vigorous efforts.

The

The ancients had a just veneration for those men by whose conduct they obtained domestic security. The Greek and Roman historians have recorded, in the most honourable terms, the patriotic citizens, who, either by their judgement or bravery, freed cities and countries from robbers and disturbers of the community.

The notion, that has been entertained by some men, " that the apprehending of highwaymen, " house-breakers, footpads, &c. by exertions pro- " fessedly directed to that end, is not honourable," is certainly not only very erroneous, because contrary to common sense, but exceedingly hurtful, for men of sentiment and honour may be deterred from engaging in such services, for fear of experiencing illiberal reflections.

That men, whose very existence may depend on preserving the secrets of thief-taking, should discountenance such brave and disinterested conduct, is not at all strange, because perfectly consistent with their designs. But it is astonishing, that gentlemen of understanding, spirit, and honour, should

adopt

adopt a notion so inimical to the interest and happiness of society!

I can now, however, with great pleasure, congratulate you on the prospect of the above prejudice being entirely removed through the exertions of the gentlemen of the Artillery-Company, whose late effectual services cannot fail of calling forth the spirit of those who disdain to be protected but by the assistance of their own arms.†

To

---

† Struck with horror at the murder of Mr. *Hurd*, and the continual robberies and acts of violence committed in the roads about Islington, a party of the gentlemen of the Honourable Artillery-Company, accompanied by peace-officers, went, for many nights, on a spirited search after the villains. They took up several very suspicious persons; and, what is worthy observation, when, on an occasion, they presented some of these to a magistrate for examination, he rebuked them for meddling with a business, which, he said, his own people much better understood.

( 24 )

To see a company of young gentlemen spurning the luxuries and frivolous enjoyments of the age, and engaging in an undertaking of danger, in which the lives and properties of their fellow-citizens are deeply concerned, must afford the most pleasing reflections to good and contemplative minds.

But, while villains are detected and vice restrained, let not public virtue go undistinguished. The human mind, I have often heard you say, must have a gratification in every pursuit Expressions of the approbation of mankind are indeed the pleasures and rewards of the laudably ambitious.

I am led to think, that, if more attention were paid to this observation, there would be a greater degree of *active* virtue in the nation.* Let the corporation

of

---

* A worthy young gentleman of the Honourable Artillery-Company, who was exceedingly active in the service of quelling the riots, in June, 1780, and has been so on every call of the chief magistrate and governors of the Bank since, and who lost his right arm by an accident from a field-piece, is a melancholy instance of neglect of merit and public spirit.

of London set the example. offering the freedom of the city to gentlemen who are not already free, and who, for their public benefits, are deserving of the most respectable alliance with the city, presenting to others medals bearing inscriptions expressive of their praise-worthy deeds, would be tokens of gratitude and approbation just and prudent in the corporation to bestow, pleasing and honourable to the gentlemen on whom they should be conferred, and productive of a glorious emulation.

I am, sir, &c.

## LETTER IV.

TO ****** ******.

SIR,

THE propositions of Mr Hanway, respecting the most important objects of police, have not been properly regarded.† It is curious to remark, of the human mind, how often it is proud of, and defends with all the strength of fallacious arguments, practices and opinions which, sooner or later, it must forego, and give up to judgement and experience.

Mr. Hanway's ideas of the efficacy of solitude in imprisonment are however at length generally admitted, though much time will be required for the abolition of prisons and methods founded on contrary opinions. The same sagacious and good mind, that imagined the benefits which might probably flow from the solitary imprisonment of depraved men, could

---

† Vide the *Citizen's Monitor*, by Jonas Hanway, Esq.

could not but apprehend and prophecy the evils that would arise from congregating them in *hulks*. ‡ Thank God! these places are to receive no more of such beings, to return them to the world *in a state worse than the first!*\* Murders and dreadful depredations, which reason and sound policy might have prevented, have brought shocking proofs of the truth of the predictions of this able reformer. The nation is now overrun with men highly finished in those schools of wickedness; and many more must yet be added to them from the same sources. Lost to all sense of humanity, expert in every artifice of villany, what is not to be dreaded from them? Every magistrate, every good citizen, is called upon to propose

‡ Mr. Hanway, in the beginning, condemned the plan of the hulks, and cautioned the public against the evils that would necessarily flow from them. When carried into execution, he enquired minutely into the discipline adopted, and suggested a conduct as much as possible to obviate and diminish the evil.

\* At the time this letter was written, it was understood that the practice of sending convicts to the hulks would be discontinued.

pose and assist in plans of defence and extermination. The gratifications of these men, which are their incentives to acts of lawless violence, require places in which they may meet and revel, and conduct their detested midnight orgies. They must convene to plan their works of deep-laid villany, the robberies of the present time are most of them committed by †large parties. They acquire confidence in society and council; a suggestion from a latent feeling of humanity, or a shudder from the last struggle of conscience, are subdued by the encouragements of a more experienced and hardened offender. According to the facility with which men can conduct any enterprize, will be their degree of progress in it. Consider the lives of these men, and suppose that the difficulty and trouble of obtaining their enjoyments by violence were rendered greater than they would be by industry in their several avocations, certainly they would

---

† In the autumn, 1784, the writer and two other gentlemen were stopped, by a gang of at least *five* footpads, (the postillion said he counted *six*,) near Ilford, in Essex.

would then be determined to courses of industry. It is true, their pleasures might still be criminal, but the means of procuring them ceasing to be so would be a lessening of the sum of vice and misery. In short, could the meetings of bad persons be prevented, an astonishing deal of evil would, of consequence, be removed, and a foundation laid for the very best system of domestic security. The conduct of those persons, who have methodized the apprehending of thieves and other infractors of the laws, is by no means calculated to prevent crimes and indiscriminately to remove criminals. The execution of *their* plans requires the agency of bad men. This is not striking at the root; on the contrary, it implies a chain of interest, from the thief to the magistrate, disgraceful to human nature, it intimates supineness and want of public spirit in men whose principles would bind them to rules of honour and impartial justice. In the city, the source of executive justice, it is presumed, is pure, though without any system, in the environs, it is to be feared, it is polluted, and so it must therefore run in all the channels of plan and system.

Magistrates should be awakened to a matter of very great importance to the peace and security of the inhabitants of this town and kingdom, namely, the haunts of house-breakers, thieves, &c. These may be considered as central spots, whence they start to seize on their prey, and to which they return to riot over their booty. An idea may be formed of these places from the substance of the following narrative of some excursions made to secure offenders after the riot, and the escape of prisoners from the jails, in the year 1780.

We were several times on this duty, attended by peace-officers, particularly two, who have been long employed in the art and mystery of thief-taking.— We visited Chick-lane, Field-lane, Black-boy alley, and other such kind of places, whence we escorted many recognized criminals to prison. The buildings in these parts constitute a sort of distinct town, or district, calculated for the reception of the darkest and most dangerous enemies to society; in which, when pursued for the commission of crimes, they easily conceal themselves, or from which, by the construction of the houses, they can as readily escape.

The houses are divided, from top to bottom, into many apartments, with doors of communication among them all, and also with the adjacent houses: some have two, others three, nay, four, doors opening into different alleys. To such a height has our neglect of police arrived, that the owners of these houses make no secret of their being let for the entainment of THIEVES! One woman, a rosy veteran, being questioned on this head, answered, *Where are they to go, if we do not admit them?* Thus they support, on principle, the propriety of maintaining the republic of thieves. In many of the rooms were six, seven, eight, nine, and ten, men in bed in one loft, into which we were obliged to creep through a trap-door, were eight men. At a certain house, near West Smithfield, reported to be employed chiefly for the reception of highwaymen and thieves, it was with difficulty we obtained admittance. At the end of a little passage, up stairs, we observed a small deal door, there we demanded to be let in, but were answered, in a rough tone of voice, *I am a half-pay officer, and will not admit you* We explained our business and authority, promising

to

to treat him with civility. At length we were admitted into a small bed-room in great disorder. From this apartment a door opened into a room which appeared to be at least fifty feet long, and proportionably broad. Here were all kinds of implements of artisans; saws, screws, various sorts of instruments for cutting, a quantity of spirit of nitre, a furnace, crucibles, burnt bones, locks, hinges, a great number of books, chests of drawers, and all in the wildest confusion. Our *half-pay officer* now assumed the style and title of *philosopher*. Not thinking it proper to take him before a magistrate, we left him to the speculation of inquirers into ambiguous characters.

The peace-officers and keepers of these houses were well acquainted with each other, and on much better terms than is compatible with the distinction between honesty and roguery. Our jealousy was increased the more, as these persons insisted there could be no motive for going into many houses, although from thence we brought away the most suspected persons, while the same officers conducted us into places where there appeared to be the least ground for suspicion, nor could they be prevailed on to go up stairs at some houses where we desired their attendance. We were sometimes inclined to think we were in the haunts of highwaymen, as well as footpads and house-breakers, for we here and there saw heaps of the bones of horses.

In obedience to your request, after my first letter, I have gone freely into reflections on the subjects of my observation. If you find me dull or injudicious in my strictures, my apology is, that, not to fail in my duty to you, I am obliged to scribble while "the "drowsy world lies lost in sleep."

Farewel !

## LETTER V.

TO ****** ******.

SIR,

THE man, who has been robbed on the highway, exclaims, " hang every highwayman " and footpad!" and, if his riches equal his desire of revenge, *he pays a thief-taker for the life of the robber*, who will then be apprehended and hanged.——— The fool, who has chosen to solace himself with a lady of Covent-garden, and has had his purse pilfered from his pocket, calls for vengeance in his turn; and Bridewel and Newgate are instantly to be filled with miserable prostitutes. ——— Early this morning, my house was violently attacked by thieves. They have broken my door to pieces. I heard them, and was presently down stairs. I suppose they saw my light, and fled. I, too, instantly felt a vindictive spirit kindling. " Mercy," said I, " should never be " shewn to house-breakers! The present plan of " watching should be abolished!" But sober reason soon informed me, this was only revenge and folly

If

If men, my good sir, were seriously to consider the true end of punishment, which is godlike, *not to destroy, but to save*, they would, doubtless, act very differently. passion would be kept within bounds, and thoughts, of calling back the corrupted members of society to a sense of social duties, and of preventing depravity in others, would fill the minds of good citizens, instead of sentiments of blood and revenge, directing to a conduct, whose tendency is to propagate, and not retard, the progress of wickedness.

Finite wisdom can never, with due accuracy, apportion punishments to the degrees and qualities of crimes. Yet there are some of so manifestly dangerous a nature, as, by universal consent of mankind, to demand extraordinary attention. Of this kind is house-breaking, and the frequency of the commission of this offence, in and about this great town, calls for a vigorous exertion of means calculated to secure the offenders, and strike terror into the minds of those who are on the brink of equal depravity and guilt.

Is it not, however, entertaining to attend to the variety of sentiments and correspondent practices, concerning the guarding against this species of criminals? One man, by bolts, bars, and locks, sets all of them at defiance, but he thinks not of the insecurity of his neighbour, who has it not in his power to fortify his castle in the like manner. Another places a blunderbuss in a window: if the thief be a fool, he may pass by this house, and go to that of a helpless woman, who may live next door, but he may as likely say, " this man is a timid creature, " and I will certainly break into his house." A third by bells and dogs proposes to call up the apprehension of a thief; and all, by rattles and cries, will desire thieves to depart, lest harm come unto them. All this seems to be founded in great complaisance and kindness to thieves. ——— Probably, if a little more of the arts, practised against a foreign enemy, were to be employed against these domestic foes, the success, in regard to the security of society, would be much greater.

The principle, of creating difficulties in the way of thieves, is undoubtedly just, and all the above means might, under different circumstances, be very properly employed. But, still, there is no one of them

them that feems to have fully in view the apprehending of houfe-breakers. I fhall fuggeft what I think might have an excellent effect.———Let each houfe, in the fame neighbourhood, have a bell placed in the chamber of the mafter, the ftring, or pull, to terminate in the chamber of the adjoining houfe, and this to be done reciprocally. Thefe bells and pulls might be fo hung, and put in fuch places, as fhould fecure them from accidental or wanton pulling. Upon an alarm of *thieves*, by ringing the bells communicating with the houfe, the rogues might be filently, and as it were by ftratagem, furrounded, and, almoft with certainty, taken.—What robbers would be hardy enough to attack a houfe, under the apprehenfion of fuch a furprize? I would recommend this expedient between your and your friend ****'s houfes in the country The wires might be carried through a leaden pipe under the road ———— I would name thefe bells RECIPROCALS

In regard to the fecuring of doors, what think you of a fmall iron wedge with two holes in it, the wedge to be placed under the door, and pins, or gimlets, paffed through the holes into the floor? The excellence

lence of this mode of fastening consists in this, that the resistence will increase with the power employed to force the door open. You often make long tours in the summer, might not these wedges be useful for the door of your chamber at an inn? You might carry a couple of them in your pocket without the least inconvenience.

Adieu!

## LETTER VI.

TO ****** ******.

SIR,

PRIDE, folly, and wickedness, actuate so many persons, that it often happens, when a man of sound judgement and stern integrity reasons abstractedly of wickedness and vice, and speaks in general terms of the relaxation or perversion of executive justice, that some one starts up, calls for facts, and triumphs over virtue if specific commissions of crimes be not immediately adduced. It has been my task to lay before you some truths that appear to me very interesting at this moment, and which will enable you to defend, with confidence, in your respectable circles, your own excellent sentiments and principles respecting offences and offenders in this great town. I wish, however, that, in pursuance of this design, I may not call up serious and constant apprehensions in your mind, for I have not yet finished my relation of thieves and their secret places.

I was

I was lately on a service that afforded me much matter for observation. Information was given to the chief magistrate, that several, of a large party of convicts that had escaped from a vessel intended to convey them to the coast of Africa, had been seen in Gravel-lane, &c. in the neighbourhood of Houndsditch † The Artillery-Company were immediately applied to for assistance, and about forty of the gentlemen marched silently from the Armory-House about two in the morning. They were joined by an alderman, one of the marshals, and some constables belonging to a justice's office. The disposition, that was made on this occasion, did certainly great credit to the active adjutant CLARK, for, at the same moment, every avenue of the district of Gravel-lane was secured, so that it would have been impossible for any person to have escaped. A detachment then searched all the houses, and though, perhaps, on any other night, numbers of the most abandoned wretches might have been here found, yet, on this occasion, so far from meeting with the objects of our research, we hardly discovered one man in the place, excepting

† In April, 1784.

excepting the keepers of houses. ——— We observed the dwellings to be constructed on the like principle of those in Chick-lane, &c. The constables also appeared to be on the most familiar terms with the landlords and landladies; hailing them in a friendly manner, winking at them, whispering and drinking drams with them. Good God! when will the eyes of my fellow-citizens be opened? When will they " take arms against a sea of *wickedness*, " and, by opposing, end *it?*" Nothing could be plainer, than that the keepers of these houses had been informed of our intended visit. My brethren of the corps will be my witnesses, that these people did not appear in the least surprised at the sight of us; but every thing had the appearance of an undertaking frustrated by the artifice of those whose duty it was to have promoted and secured its success.

Who can say how many of these harbouring places there are in this town?

Since the above, I have attended on another service which brought additional proof of our insecurity. The lord-mayor having received information of a

gang of thieves being at a public house in a court in Bishopsgate-street, a small detachment of the Artillery-Company, accompanied by a marshal and some turnkeys from the Poultry-compter, went thither at midnight. We truly surprised them in the midst of their revelry, and handcuffed and conducted to prison a greater number of dangerous and suspicious persons than what formed our detachment. The ladies in their company were numerous, and of the most depraved class; they were strongly disposed to fight for their paramours; and the mob, that soon collected, appeared as inclined to assist them. But there is a magic in a red coat, which every magistrate ought well to understand. For, although Englishmen will ever, I trust, abhor the interposition of the military in the civil department of government, when not absolutely necessary, yet it does not follow that this remark might not be usefully applied when the services of *armed citizens* should be required. On the contrary, it might be the means of rendering the assistance of the regular forces on any occasion unnecessary.——
In this business there was no intrigue; an honest city-officer, with two men, from a prison, who were

ignorant

ignorant of the enterprize, did their duty, and, perhaps, prevented many robberies, &c at least for a few nights. But what will a sober citizen say, when informed, that the people of this very public house were suffered to retain a licence?

The following occurrences seem equally curious and interesting. ———— A man was brought to the London-Hospital, who had been shot in the breast in endeavouring to break into a house he got well, was tried, and acquitted of the charge of burglary. He was afterwards pointed out to me, by a worthy and sensible Jew gentleman, in Duke's Place, dressed very splendidly. My friend remarked, " that he " knew him well, that he had not any known means " of getting a living, and that he was acquainted " with many other characters, among his people, of " a similar description." I observed, it was a pity that some plan could not be devised for the regulation of the lower order of Jews, and restraining them from becoming accomplices in, and perpetrators of, crimes He replied, " He was certain that the " respectable part of the body would do all in their " power, and be happy, to advance such a good de-
" sign,

"sign; but that the undertaking would be far
"more arduous than what I might imagine;
"for, he believed, there was hardly a robbery,
"to any confiderable amount, in which many of
"thefe perfons were not, either directly or remotely,
"concerned. That fome of them had crucibles
"and furnaces always ready for melting down gold
"and filver, others were continually employed, in
"different parts of the kingdom, in difpofing of
"ftolen property, while yet others were fent to
"Holland, and various foreign parts, to get rid of
"articles which cannot be fafely or advantageoufly
"expofed and fold in this country." He added,—
"that the neighbourhood of Houndfditch was the
"principal feat of thefe gentry."

Put all thefe circumftances together, and we have the great lines of a dreadful *fyftem* of depredation, againft which we have no fyftem of defence and fecurity; for I cannot confider that as a fyftem which has not refpect to every radical and great caufe of the evils deplored.———Without an adequate remedy,

very

very soon employed, thieves will become our law-givers!

Adieu!

LETTER

## LETTER VII.

TO ****** ******,

SIR,

THERE are practices in this town, and which seem to be authorised by some rulers of parishes, that do not comport with the boasted humanity of this nation. ———— Very lately, a poor black fellow was turned out of a cart on the pavement, in a parish of this city, and there left. His condition was truly shocking, for both his legs were in a state of complete mortification, he was too ill to relate the story of his sorrows. The first suggestion was, to remove him a little farther, out of the parish, lest it should be burdened with him. A more humane and intelligent person remarked, " that his " life had already been nearly sacrificed to this saving " principle, and that he would relieve them of their " concern," and instantly had him put into a coach, and conveyed to the London-Hospital. Both his legs were amputated, and the poor fellow now begs about the eastern parts of this town.

A little

A little time since, a miserable woman laid herself down at my door. She said, she had dragged her tottering frame from Portsmouth. Her appearance, one would have thought, would have melted any heart. She was reduced to the lowest state, by disease, want, and fatigue. one of her arms, from these causes, was beginning to mortify  A neighbouring SAGE came, and advised me " to have her " put away only about a hundred yards, and she " would then be out of the parish, and no expence " could accrue from her." Shocking expedient! and what, then, is to become of this sinking creature? Tossed from parish to parish, where is to be the *last* cruel scene of her existence? No, while the gates of the LONDON-HOSPITAL continue open to the diseased and wretched, we will implore the blessings of that place, to rescue from death, or to soften its pangs! She was conveyed thither  but the powers of nature were too far spent, she lived only about ten days. —— Her sense of gratitude, for what had been done for her, was so great, that she hardly ever ceased, night and day, praying for and blessing the charity.

But,

But, ah! my friend, I have a tale of woe to relate that must deeply affect your sensibility.—— A fine male infant was laid at the door of our friend, *** His good lady was from home, and he at a loss, for the instant, how to act for the preservation of the babe. An officer of the parish, who had been informed of the matter, came officiously, and assured our friend that he would take care of the business. He took up the little innocent, and went away. He looked up and down the street; and presently saw a female, of about nineteen years of age, walking to and fro, in seemingly great agitation. He contrived to have the heart-rent girl brought into a public house. He presented the child, and asked "whether she were the mother of it?"— Maternal tears were then big in her eyes! but SHAME would combat with NATURE! she replied, " No." All the while, nature spake in every anxious look on the babe, yearning for the breast. ——— The unfeeling monster proceeded, " Then I will lay " it in the kennel." She shrieks, seizes the infant, and flies from her enemy, MAN!——Whither, hapless female, wilt thou go? Would that a STERNE, or a SHENSTONE, or a HANWAY, or that thou, my honoured friend, hadst been near, to have comforted her broken heart! And what are her crimes, say, rigid stoic, that her tender nature should be so violently treated? Alas! her heart was too susceptible: she loved, was deceived, and undone! And wilt thou, seducer, bear no share of the burden of her woe? Whither, hapless female, wilt thou flee? Perhaps, distracted, she may plunge herself and babe into some stream, or she may dash out the brains of the smiling boy, saying, " I will not add to the race " of savages," and rave out her remaining days in Bedlam!

But let us finish this affecting story. The officer returns, runs over the relation of the circumstances, and adds, " She is now out of the " parish, and we are safe." " A curse light on " thee!" said my friend.

I am, &c.

# LETTER VII.

## TO ****** ******.

SIR,

THE relating of the story of the unfortunate girl and child, which concluded my last, affected me so much, that I could not then proceed.

You will certainly admit, that the conduct which I have set forth, must not only be productive of MISERY, but also lead directly to CRIMES. Not that I conceive child-murder to be nearly so frequent a crime as is by some imagined, for I cannot believe, that *shame* and *false reasoning* can easily destroy the strongest tie of nature. But prostitution, distraction, abject poverty, theft, and their dreadful consequences, must flow from not casting an eye of pity, early, on the forsaken, the diseased, and distressed.

For what description of objects was the LONDON WORKHOUSE designed?——— If there be no place to which miserable beings can be sent, for temporary relief, until their settlements be found, or they can

be

be admitted into some hospitable dwelling suitable to their circumstances, it is surely right that such a design should be established. The inhabitants *in general* being contributory to its support, there would cease to be a desire of *shuffling* a poor wretch from one parish to another, and relief, according to exigences, would be instantly afforded.— The elegance, convenience, and peace, of the city, both by day and night, would be hence promoted, the national character of humanity justified, and the sum of vice and misery lessened.

You enquire, " what are my observations con-
" cerning the unhappy women who croud our
" streets; and the situation, &c. of public houses in
" this town?" These are, indeed, important subjects of inquiry.———— I have observed, in a former letter, " That the sensual gratifications of bad
" men are their incentives to lawless acts," and
" that their enjoyments and criminal designs require
" proper places, in which they may meet, and re-
" vel, and hold council against the peace of so-
" ciety." If these be facts, whence the infatuation that no effectual measures are pursued for clearing

our streets of prostitutes, and removing every improper public house? — Yet humanity shudders at the common mode of treatment of these wretched females!
" Surely the HAPPINESS, not to mention the virtue,
" or utility to society, of such a multitude of indi-
" viduals, is an object which calls loudly for the in-
" terposition of the legislature "† Having holden a professional office at the MAGDALEN-HOSPITAL for near ten years, I am enabled to form some idea of the female character in a state of lost innocence, and I believe there are few who might not, by properly-appropriated means, be considerably mended. If we cannot make a saint, shall we not try to mend a sinner? The sensible magistrate says "Yes," yet continues to congregate these poor wretches in BRIDE-WELL or other prisons; not with the least reasonable prospect of *mending a sinner*, but indeed with a certainty of putting away intirely the little sense of SHAME or DELICACY that may possibly hang to the heart, and preparing them for crimes of a new kind and a higher degree!

---

† Vide Female Tuition, or an Address to Mothers on the Education of their Daughters, p. 236.

degree!——Many a lost daughter, sister, and friend, has the above institution restored to their families, to honour, and the world! Let our magistrates imitate the *spirit* of that excellent charity. let it be the special business of proper persons to enquire *minutely* into the circumstances of those brought before them, and to proceed in the treatment of them accordingly. Applications to their parents, friends, or parishes, might then be made, and, till these measures were taken, they should be lodged in *separate* apartments, and be attended by a divine. The good impressions, received during this period of solitary confinement, might produce the fruit of good works, even at a distant time, and when little understood.

Nothing, sir, has surprised me more than the number of public houses in *by-lanes, alleys, courts,* and *the most obscure places* of this town. Not one public house, so situated, should be suffered. There cannot be offered an apology for admitting them. At best, they can be considered only as tippling-houses, but, to my certain knowledge, they are, many of them, places of harbour for pick-pockets, thieves, and house-breakers, and all of them are

strongly

strongly to be suspected. —— Such was the house in Bishopsgate-street; and so situated are all the public houses in the districts of Chick-lane, &c.

I am, &c.

## LETTER VIII.

### TO ****** ******.

SIR,

I Agree with you in opinion, that, in the government of this city, we may observe great inattention to many very important matters. Why, for instance, does not the CORPORATION provide an adequate guard for the BANK, admitting that a guard there be necessary? As friends to the liberties of the people, and the rights of citizens, they should reflect on the use bad men might make of the present practice of mounting guard at that place. Suppose, at some period, either a monarchical, or, which is more to be apprehended, an aristocratical, tyranny were to endeavour to destroy the liberties of Englishmen —— The CAPITAL would be the first object of *dread* or *hope*. But the precedent of the Bank-guard would greatly favour the wicked design, for it might afford a pretext for making a GARRISON of *every* PUBLIC OFFICE, and thus, by art and insidious means, to effect what avowed intention and open violence could

never

never have atchieved. But you will readily suggest many reasons why the treasure contained in the Bank should not be intrusted to the care of *common mercenary troops*. Surely, sir, a plan might be formed for establishing a respectable, safe, and constitutional, guard at this place, and, till that were done, some expedient should be adopted for maintaining the city's PRIVILEGES. Would it not, at least, be proper that the guard should be occasionally withdrawn, in *acknowlegement* of those privileges? I have been led to these reflections from having received a summons to attend at the Bank this night. You know, that, by law, the king's troops are not to be in any city or town during the time of an election of a member of parliament. — This day the election commenced in the city; and, during its continuance, detachments of the Artillery-Company will do duty at the Bank.

I wish the instance adduced had been the only proof of inattention in our magistrates, but many others might be mentioned.—Their integrity none will dare to dispute.

The omissions of these gentlemen seem to arise principally from their dwelling out of the city,

city, being little in it, and leaving the concerns of the several wards nearly altogether to deputies. — Can this be called watching over the peace and prosperity of the city?

When superiors in office become negligent, relaxation of duty will take place in every subordinate department. If the ALDERMEN be supine, the DEPUTIES and COMMON-COUNCIL will hardly be very active: the integrity and efficiency of CONSTABLES will be disregarded the WATCHMEN will prove old or infirm, will sleep instead of watch, will be off their stands, or not heedful in them, or suffer felony to be committed near at hand, because *not in their beat!* ———— This is human nature, and a general idea of the defects of city-government.

When will the corporation solemnly take up the consideration of the security of the lives and property of their constituents? When the propositions of the patriotic and spirited Alderman TURNER † were rejected

---

† Vide a Plan for rendering the Militia of London useful and respectable, &c

rejected, a committee was appointed to deliberate on the subject of a reform in the militia and watch. Has that committee made any report? If the present municipal laws be equal to the end required, why are not measures taken for the effectual execution of them? If inadequate, let the city-members propose new ones to parliament, and let PEACE be in all our streets, and VIRTUE, as well as riches, render our city glorious!

Adieu!

## LETTER IX.

### TO ****** ******.

SIR,

OUR good friend, ******, has favoured me with a copy of our excellent RECORDER's opinion on the question of the *Legality of the* LONDON MILITARY FOOT-ASSOCIATION. It contains so much constitutional information, and is written with such great strength and perspicuity, that I am sure the reading of it will afford you high satisfaction.

"IT is a matter of some difficulty to define the precise limits and extent of the rights of the people of this realm to bear arms, and to instruct themselves in the use of them, *collectively*, and much more so to point out all the acts of that kind, which would be illegal or doubtful in their nature.

"The right of his majesty's Protestant subjects, to have arms for their own defence, and to use them for lawful purposes, is most clear and undeniable. It seems, indeed, to be considered, by the ancient laws of this kingdom, not only as a *right*, but as a *duty*; for all the subjects of the realm, who are able to bear arms, are bound to be ready, at all times, to assist the sheriff, and other civil magistrates, in the execution of the laws and the preservation of the public peace. And that this right, which every Protestant most unquestionably possesses *individually*, may, and in many cases *must*, be exercised *collectively*, is likewise a point which I conceive to be most clearly established by the authority of judicial decisions and ancient acts of parliament, as well as by reason and common sense

" From the proposition, that the possession and the use of arms, to certain purposes, is lawful, it seems to follow, of necessary consequence, that it cannot be unlawful *to learn to use them* (for such lawful purposes) with *safety and effect* For, it would be too gross an absurdity to allege, that it is *not lawful to be instructed in the use of* any thing which it is *lawful to use*; and, by the same mode of reasoning, from the right of using arms, in some cases, collectively and in *bodies*, follows the right of being collectively, as well as individually,

dividually, *instructed* in the use of them, if it be true, which I apprehend it most clearly is, that the safe and effectual use of arms in collective bodies cannot be taught to separate individuals

" Thus far, I think, we advance on firm and solid ground. But here the difficulty commences; for it may be asked " If the right of being *collectively* in-
" structed in the use of arms is admitted in its full ex-
" tent, would it be lawful for a vast multitude, to
" the amount of many thousand armed men, without
" any visible occasion or apparent lawful object, un-
" authorised by government or any magistrate, to as-
" semble together, and march where they pleased,
" for the purpose, as they professed, of instructing
" and exercising themselves in the use of arms?"
To this question, *stated in these unlimited terms*, I should certainly answer in the negative; because, in my opinion, an affirmative answer would amount to a dissolution of all government and a subversion of all law.

" Where, then, shall we draw the line? or how
" define the number and manner of assembling to
" exercise

" exercise in the use of arms, which shall determine
" such an act to be legal or otherwise?"

" To this I answer, that the best consideration I can give the subject does not enable me to draw any such *precise line*, or to lay down any proposition respecting the legality of armed societies, which will hold true, *at all times and in all cases, without qualification or restriction.* The circumstances of the case must, in my opinion, decide upon the legality of every such meeting. It is clearly necessary, that the *professed purpose and object* of such a society *shall be lawful*, and that they shall, at all times, when assembled, demean themselves in a peaceable and orderly manner, conformably to their professed purpose; for every breach of the peace would receive high aggravation from the circumstance of being committed by a *body of armed men*. It is, in my opinion, farther necessary, that the number of such a society shall not manifestly and greatly *exceed the professed objects of their institution*; and that they shall not, in any case, except for the suppression of sudden, violent, and *felonious*, breaches of the peace, proceed to *act* without *the authority of the civil magistrate.* With these restrictions,

restrictions, I am clearly of opinion that it is lawful, and, in many cases, highly meritorious, for the Protestant subjects of this realm to instruct themselves in the use of arms in private orderly societies.

" The lawful purposes, for which arms may be used, (besides immediate self-defence,) are, the suppression of violent and *felonious* breaches of the peace, the assistance of the civil magistrate in the execution of the laws, and the defence of the kingdom against foreign invaders. Whenever these occasions occur, the use of arms becomes not only the right, but the duty, of every Protestant able to bear them. And I have already given my opinion, that, under certain restrictions, it cannot be unlawful so to instruct themselves as to be prepared to act on those lawful occasions. The two first of these, the suppression of sudden and *felonious riots*, and the assistance of the civil magistrate, properly belong to every subject, as a member of the CIVIL state, and no commission from the crown is, in my opinion, either *necessary* or *proper*, to enable them to act for those purposes ——— As to the third, though it is the duty of every man to assist, in the most effectual manner that he can, in

the

the general defence of his country, yet, in the modern fyftem of war, the ordinary *civil* power of the ftate is become fo completely and manifeftly inadequate to the refiftance of foreign invaders, that the defence of the country againft them is more immediately intrufted to the *military*, which, in every country of Europe, is become a kind of *feparate ftate*, or body, fubject to different regulations and governed by different laws from the reft of the people, and which, fortunately, can, in this country, derive its exiftence from parliament alone. It feems, therefore, to me, that, when men are called upon, by their duty, to act againft foreign enemies, they become, in fome degree, a part of the *military ftate* for fo long as the occafion continues, and therefore ought, properly and regularly, to act under commiffion from the crown or under the command of fome of the king's officers the king being, by the conftitution, the legal commander of *the whole military force* of the country. In any other fituation, but that of invafion by a foreign enemy, I fhould very much doubt not only the *propriety*, but the *legality*, of

any

any commissions, granted by the crown to armed associations, not previously voted by parliament.

" To apply these principles to the case of the London Association I can see nothing in their plan or conduct which can justly be considered as a violation of the laws. The marching, indeed, in military array, to distant places, is in itself a doubtful act; but all doubtful acts are to be explained by the concomitant circumstances, and the apparent motives and conduct of the parties, which rule of construction, I conceive, would free the body in question from all imputation

" To strengthen the *civil power*, and to keep themselves at all times prepared for a vigorous and effectual discharge of their duty, as citizens, in supporting and assisting the civil magistrates, especially the sheriffs, in the execution of the laws, are, in my opinion, sufficient *visible* and *legal* objects for the continuance of their association. And I should, myself, rather incline to recommend it to them, and every other armed Association, to make *those* their immediate and avowed objects, and to consider themselves entirely as a part of the CIVIL, and not the *mili-*

*tary*, power of the state in the latter capacity, they *must*, in my opinion, however their commissions might be framed, be subject to the *military command* of the crown, in the former, they neither need nor ought to be subject to *that* command, or to any other, except that of the civil magistrate, to which, in certain cases, all are subject.

" The effect of *general commissions* from the crown would certainly subject all acting under their authority to the *mutiny-act*, and the whole of the *military law*, while they continued to act under that authority, and also to the military rules respecting *resignations*, which I do not conceive to be quite *optional* to the parties, and I do not apprehend that any declaration or promise, accompanying such *general* commissions, could be effectual in preventing their necessary legal operation.

As to the effect, which *special, limited, and conditional*, commissions might have, it must depend so much on the particular wording of them, the practice of the war-office in granting them, and other circumstances of which I am not sufficiently informed, ed, that I cannot undertake to give my opinion upon it.

For these reasons, added to the doubts I have already expressed as to the *legality* of *military commissions* not founded on the authority of parliament, I would again recommend it to this respectable body, to consider themselves as a CIVIL, and not a *military, association*, and confine themselves, in the present state of things, to those *civil objects* which will, upon the principles before laid down, sufficiently justify them *in exercising, and perfecting themselves in the use of arms*, without any commission whatever. Nor will they, in fact, by this means, lose sight of that which was the original object of their meeting; for this mode of proceeding will equally qualify them to serve their king and country, with vigour and effect, if their duty should call them to assist in repelling a foreign enemy, in which case, should it happen, they might, and I think ought to, apply for, and act under, the king's commission, and would, I dare say, have no objection to subject themselves to military law for so long as an enemy was in the kingdom, and, if special commissions should at any time be

applied

applied for by the Association, I can see no objection to their being so framed as *to take place only upon the landing of an enemy* in the country, and *to remain in force only* during the continuance of such an invasion."†

Farewel!

† Dated July 24, 1780.

# AN ESSAY

ON THE MEANS OF

## PREVENTING CRIMES

AND

## AMENDING CRIMINALS.

# AN ESSAY

## On the Means of PREVENTING CRIMES and AMENDING CRIMINALS.

---

O thou ! by whose almighty nod the scale
Of empire rises, or, alternate, falls,
Send forth the saving virtues round the land
In bright patrol.
THOMSON.

---

IN this country, so highly favoured by Providence, the great objects of regard, as to our *immediate* security and comfort, are FIRE and THIEVES; for the wooden walls of old England, while there are virtue and wisdom in ministers, and bravery and union among the people, will ever keep *foreign* ENEMIES from our dwellings.

The state of the nation, at this time, in respect of the latter of these EVILS, is such as calls for the most serious attention.

Is it not possible to render the lives and property of Englishmen secure from violence, to banish crimes, and make this beautiful island the SEAT of VIRTUE and LOYALTY, as it is of FREEDOM and the ARTS? The *bulk* of the inhabitants does not seem too unwieldy for the influence of good laws, and there are no *forests*, or *wilds*, or *caves*, to which infractors can flee, and escape the vigilance of justice.

But of what avail are the best laws, if not understood, or, though understood, if not impartially and spiritedly executed? *Possunt, quia posse videntur.* It is an inquiry worthy our ablest statesmen and lawyers, Whether the increase of criminals be owing to defects of law, or faults of magistrates? If to the latter, let not the venerable DESIGN of magistracy, that appears to be woven in the CONSTITUTION of this country, be in the least affected; but let proper measures be taken to have such men appointed to the honourable office of magistrate as shall execute the laws with firmness, with honour, and effect

Nor does this appear to be a very difficult task. — Were government to commence the business of reform

form at the proper place, and purfue it regularly through all the gradations of office, good and active magiftrates would foon appear, and the wifdom of the legiflature be acknowledged in the efficacy of the laws.

The LORD-LIEUTENANTS of counties, it appears, were originally appointed for purpofes very important to the PEACE and SECURITY of the inhabitants of the realm, although, at prefent, there are few who feem to confider their office in any other view than as conducive to their own aggrandifement, and parliamentary intereft in the counties over which they prefide,

The EVILS, that branch from *minifterial arts and intrigues for obtaining majorities in parliament*, have nearly ruined this country. They pervade all ranks the VICES of the GREAT, and the CRIMES of the VULGAR, have hence their radical caufe.

The appointment of LORD-LIFUTENANTS and the nomination of MAGISTRATES have, undoubtedly, been too generally derived from the fource of *parliamentary corruption* hence the want of *integrity* in fome magiftrates, of *zeal* in others, and the indignation of the friends of JUSTICE, of ORDER, and good government.

The adducing facts, in proof of this assertion, would appear invidious, nor could it be done without disrespect to some characters of high rank, whose private virtues and general tenor of conduct claim our sincere respect and esteem.

Besides, I have no doubt but the present MINISTER will trample on VENALITY  The influence of his zeal and bright example may do wonders! Providence may again smile on us, and we may again be a happy, because a virtuous, people.— Relying, therefore, on the integrity and wisdom of the minister, I shall not presume to suggest any measure for exciting PUBLIC VIRTUE in the LORD-LIEUTENANTS of counties, lest I should happily think with him, and thus lessen the dignity and effect of his conduct.

Admitting, then, that these high officers are made sensible of their duties, and have determined to exert themselves for the good of their several counties, what is the first step they ought to take? Undoubtedly, instantly to expunge from commission every man
who

who is dependent; whose time and attention are engaged in business, who is ignorant, who lives by granting warrants, who is suspected,—for a magistrate, like CÆSAR's wife, *should not be suspected.* And let them invite, and animate to exertion, men of probity, fortune, learning, and spirit —— If the INSTRUMENTS of justice were thus rendered *pure* and *fit*, the work, of preventing crimes and amending criminals, would not, I am persuaded, be found nearly so difficult as is generally imagined

But there is another *county*-officer, who also has been considered less as a CONSERVATOR of the PEACE than as a promoter of *parliamentary interest.*

" At the beginning," says Chief-Justice FINEUX, " all the administration of justice was in one hand, " namely, in the crown, then, after the multiplica- " tion of the people, that administration was distri- " buted into counties, and the *power* was committed " to a deputy in each county, namely, the viscount, " or SHERIFF, who was the king's deputy to pre- " serve the PEACE, &c " Let the SHERIFFS be required to have regard to their proper duties. let them be informed, that they are not only *impowered*, by law, to raise the *posse comitatus,* but *obliged* to do it; in all cases requiring the power of the county for maintaining peace and order. Let us imitate the example of our sister-kingdom in what is praise-worthy. In Ireland, offenders can hardly escape the vigilance of the sheriffs and the *posse comitatus.*

We will next suppose, that magistrates and sheriffs are proper men, ready to discharge their duties, and to receive advice from every well-meaning man. This, then, is the counsel, that, with deference and sincerity, I would offer.

I shall not mention many particulars necessary to be considered by the good magistrate, but shall rather confine myself to *my own* observations. Nor shall I attempt drawing a line of distinction between the means of preventing crimes and amending criminals. Reflection will shew, that the preventing one man from committing a crime may prove the mending of many criminals, and *vice versa.*

1. Let every magistrate read and well consider that excellent work of H. FIELDING, Esq *An Enquiry into the Causes of the late Increase of Robbers,* &c. This will

will afford them many admirable hints, and directions for their conduct.

2. Let the RISING GENERATION be particularly regarded. Men do not well confider in how fhort a time fociety fhall reap the fruit of good or bad feeds of education in the child that now but lifps! ———— Notwithftanding the many excellent defigns, for training up our poor children in the ways of RIGHTEOUSNESS, it is plain fomething is ftill wanting. Whether SUNDAY-SCHOOLS may fupply this deficiency I cannot prefume to fay, but every rational means, of improving the morals of the lower order of people, and this, as one, ought undoubtedly to be attempted.

3. Every PUBLIC HOUSE, not warranted by confiderations of utility and original intention, fhould be certainly abolifhed. ———— The obfervations of the learned Dr. DISNEY, in his CHARGE, on the evils arifing from thefe reforts of the idle and vicious, where the PASSIONS are raifed and REASON is obfcured, deferve the moft ferious attention. I need not add how neceffary it is frequently and minutely to inquire into the conduct of PUBLICANS. Collufions,

fions, in *granting* as well as obtaining licences, have undoubtedly been common; they should be enquired into, and guarded against.

There are public houses, in the neighbourhood of St. GEORGE's FIELDS and ISLINGTON-ROAD, that are *directly* calculated for promoting every kind of VICE. Let the sincerity of magistrates appear by the instant abolition of these places.

It is computed, there are *four thousand* public houses in Middlesex and Westminster. If an additional duty of 1l. 19s. were laid on ale-licences, making, with the present sum, 3l. it might not only be one means of shutting up many low public houses,† but, if so appropriated, perhaps produce the sum required by the 10th paragraph.

It has been remarked, that *gin-shops*, under the title of *coffee-houses*, &c. &c. have lately considerably increased.

4. It is conceived much good might arise from pawnbrokers being licensed by the justices in their divisions,

---

† I am obliged to an ingenious friend in the commission for this suggestion and that one marked † in the following page.

divisions, each paying 10l per ann. for his licence, the duty of 5l. per ann. for dealing in plate being abrogated †

5. More attention should be paid to the religion and morals of the inhabitants of the great HOSPITALS in this town. When we consider the vast number of the poor that go into these places, and that the hour of affliction is the best time for admonition, we cannot but think that these institutions might be rendered highly contributory to the great work of reformation

6 Let *beggars* and *vagabonds* of every description be secured, and dealt with according to law, having strict regard to their miseries, and the intention of the law respecting vagrants, *the prevention of crimes.*

7 Every means for promoting INDUSTRY, and affording ready employment for the poor, should be suggested. The nation would be benefited *negatively* by the application of the IDLE, though no seemingly *direct* advantage were derived from their work.

8 The labours of those philanthropists, Mr. HANWAY and Mr HOWARD, have so fully explained the BENEFITS that would result to society

from

from the SOLITARY confinement of prisoners, that I shall not enlarge on the subject. Let all good men unite in endeavours for obtaining this great DESIDERATUM of SOUND POLICY!

9. CONVICTS, if not sent out of the kingdom, should be placed in a distant part of it. Next to the evil of *congregating* them in the HULKS is that of their vicinity to the metropolis. They, at present, I am informed, cost government more than 20l. each per ann —Might they not be employed on the *wastelands*, to the great benefit of the nation in a variety of views?——But, were they placed at a considerable distance from the town, they could not readily, when discharged, return to it and their former associates, there would be a greater chance of their falling into ways of honest industry, and, in case of becoming offenders again, of being secured.

10. Handsome rewards should be granted for apprehending persons guilty of *petty* crimes, that measures might be taken, if possible, to reclaim them, and prevent them from becoming *capital* offenders. ——— It now appears as if we thirsted only for BLOOD. How many, alas! might have

have been saved, if THIEF-TAKERS had been paid as much for securing a BEGINNER in wickedness as for the *finished* robber, and that means of *melioration* had been employed.

## IN THE COUNTIES.

Let a COMMITTEE of SECURITY, consisting of        persons, freeholders if possible, be appointed, by the inhabitants, in every town in the kingdom. They should choose a chairman, who ought to be a magistrate. Their duties should be to take cognizance of every thing respecting the security of the inhabitants within their district, to keep a record of their proceedings, to be reported to the justices at the QUARTER-SESSIONS. and, from the information conveyed by the several reports, and the journals that should be kept by the keepers of prisons, the justices might determine on measures for the peace and security of the *whole* county. All expences should be defrayed by the county ———— This plan would, I believe, excite public spirit, and greatly promote the good designs of magistracy.

## IN THE CITY OF LONDON.

I would propose, that one hundred and fifty men, able and of character, be kept constantly in pay. That thirty good horses be provided. That arms and accoutrements be prepared for thirty horsemen and twenty foot. That they be properly officered; and, particularly, that the first and second officers be amply paid, and totally detached from other avocations. Fifty men to do duty every night, viz. thirty horse and twenty foot. GUILDHALL to be the *head-quarters*. Their duties to be, to patrole the streets, to keep constables and watchmen on their duty; to apprehend criminals, assist at fires, and prevent or remove disturbances and enormities of every kind.

They should every day report to the magistrates the proceedings of the previous night.——A record should be kept of these reports, and of those from the keepers of prisons; and, from them, general instructions should be given, from time to time, to the SUPERINTENDANT-GENERAL of the CITY-GUARD.

I am

I am firmly persuaded, that the effects of this simple expedient would prove astonishingly great, not only in the several views mentioned, but also *in terrorem* to evil-minded persons of every description.

I have purposely avoided minute matters for, if these hints should be thought worthy of attention, a committee must be appointed for deliberating on the subject and systematizing a plan.

I am aware that the authority of the legislature would be required for enforcing some of the regulations proposed, but there can be no doubt of the assent of parliament to measures founded on the experience of respectable magistrates, and calculated to promote the security and happiness of the subject.

I cannot conclude without remarking, that reflections on the subject of crimes bring irrefragable proofs of the *natural* tendency of man to offend against his GOD and his *fellow-creatures*, and of the *necessity*, as well as the *power* and *beauty*, of RELIGION, in making him contribute to *peace and good will on earth*, and in preparing him for a happy IMMORTALITY!

## THE END.